HOW TO BE A BETTER WIFE

Becoming a spontaneous and fun wife for your husband

Emily Chapman

INTRODUCTION

15 standards Of A Decent Spouse

In a general public like our own with its "clash of the genders", sex exchanging, and the ascent of the young lady manager it's more confounding than any time in recent memory to make sense of being a decent spouse. However there is as yet a craving in us to be one! That is the reason endless ladies today feel lost, wanting to be esteemed and have significance, and it never gets fulfilled in light of the fact that they don't have the foggiest idea what their identity was made to be.

The standards I'm going to impart to you have been the sign of a decent spouse for a huge number of years and they'll show you how to be the lady your man pines for. I'm going to show you precisely being a decent spouse.

Marriage is cooperation. What's more, it requires both the accomplices to invest in their individual amounts of energy to make things work. Similarly as you would need a 'great spouse', your significant other would need a decent wife. Present day, dynamic ladies may make some extreme memories tolerating the possibility of a 'great spouse'. Be that as it may, pause. Try not to bounce to seething determinations that being a decent spouse is tied in with making a cliché persona of a wedded lady.

Principes Of A Decent Spouse: There is nobody size-fits-all answer for being a decent wife. In any case, there are sure things you ought to and ought not do in a relationship to be an extraordinary accomplice. Here, I have list down a couple of character attributes that can make you a decent spouse.

CHAPTER ONE

Express your adoration

Do you love your better half? Do you feel cheerful and safe when you are with him? On the off chance that you have resolved to go through a lifetime with a man through pre-marriage ceremony, you should cherish him. Be that as it may, cherishing isn't sufficient. A relationship flourishes with the declaration of that adoration, among different feelings. So on the off chance that you love your better half, let him know and give him the amount he intends to you. You don't need to make expound articulations of adoration consistently. It could simply be little signals, for example, a kiss or a kiss on the cheek every so often, or making his preferred breakfast on occasion or picking a film he jumps at the chance to observe together.

Impart

In any relationship, correspondence is basic. What's more, marriage is no exemption. Discard the confused thoughts that an accomplice should recognize what the other one thinks and needs. Your better half can't understand minds, similarly as you can't. You may think about every others' preferences and inclinations yet not really what they are thinking or feeling. Open correspondence in the marriage implies that you mention to your significant other what you think or feel and what you expect of him. Converse with your better half – ask, say, and talk about. Evade the quiet treatment, which can compound the situation. Try not to leave your better half speculating about what you need, and abstain from accepting or envisioning things about his conduct.

Be steady

Be it a profession, a leisure activity or whatever else that your significant other seeks after, he'd need and need your help. Being strong in a marriage isn't just about being there when the accomplice is struggling. It is tied in with acknowledging or commending him when he accomplishes an achievement, or when he beats his dread and has a go at something new. Supporting isn't continually expressing beneficial things. It is likewise about contribution productive analysis to urge him to improve in whatever he is doing. For instance, being steady of your significant other's new business thought when you are monetarily agreeable is a decent method to help his certainty and reinforce the relationship.

CHAPTER TWO

Be his closest companion

The best marriage is where the couple is each other's closest companion. Nothing is better than being enamored with your closest companion. This is an affection that is profound, solid and veritable. Permit a sound fellowship to create among you and your significant other, and see what improvement it makes to your life.

Regard the individual he is

The best relationships are those where the accomplices regard one another. Your better half is his own person, with defects what not. Regard the individual he is, not for what he accomplishes for you or the family. Shared regard in the marriage is an absolute necessity. This reflects in the manner you talk and carry on with one another. Try not to disparage, mortify, strike or damage your significant other, regardless of whether in private or open. A bit of prodding is okay, however offending isn't alright. So watch what you state and think before you talk.

Show an enthusiasm for his inclinations

Not all that your significant other preferences could intrigue you. You don't need to do things that he prefers, yet give your significant other the space to seek after his inclinations and give some interest in what he's doing. Get some information about the game, book or pastime that he is keen on. Do a little schoolwork and find out about the things he is keen on so you can have a discussion about that as well.

CHAPTER THREE

Regard his requirement for space

'Space' is an idea that couple of individuals comprehend. Each individual needs their own space. Indeed, even wedded men need their space on occasion and might need to withdraw to their man-cavern. Regard that and give him some space, and permit him to seek after his diversions and interests. Confining your companion's opportunity and space can be choking for them and negatively affect the relationship.

Tune in

Listening is basic for powerful correspondence, and maybe more significant than talking. So put forth a cognizant attempt to hear, yet tune in and comprehend when your significant other is talking. Focus on him during a discussion. Set aside your telephone, turn off the television or turn down the music that could be diverting you. Giving your significant other your complete consideration when he is talking shows the amount you regard him. Listening doesn't mean you need to concur with him. Yet, even to dissent, you should tune in to what he is stating.

Be grateful

Men, as well, like to be cherished, acknowledged and commended. Disclose to him the amount you value the seemingly insignificant details he accomplishes for you, for the kids or in the house. Commendation urges him to support you, and furthermore sends the message that his endeavors are perceived. You don't need to praise him enthusiastically to show appreciation. A straightforward, certifiable 'thank you' will do the trick.

CHAPTER FOUR

Start the correct quarrel

Are you are aware of any hitched couple that doesn't battle? Marriage is around two extraordinary, one of a kind people who will have contrasts. The contradictions and contrasts can in some cases lead to battles. What's more, those battles, if too much, can strain the relationship. That doesn't mean you bargain unfailingly. No. It implies you need to think and start your quarrel shrewdly. Ask yourself – 'Is it worth battling for?' What's preventing you from trading off and let your significant other have his direction now and again? In the event that it's an inconsequential issue, released it. Try not to let your personality come in the method of a cheerful, cherishing relationship with the man you love.

Be straightforward

Trustworthiness is the base for a confiding in relationship. Relationships that keep going depend on genuineness and open correspondence, with a bad situation for cheating or lying. Your better half merits genuineness and honesty from you, similarly as you do from him. Being honest won't generally be simple. Now and again your genuineness may disturb your significant other and may even prompt battles. In any case, contemptibility can harm a relationship so much that the accomplices will make some extreme memories confiding in one another once more. One untruth or selling out and your better half may consistently have a waiting uncertainty about your honesty.

Be your actual self

On the off chance that you are not happy with what your identity is, you won't be open to uncovering your actual self to your accomplice. Be your actual self in a relationship, directly from the earliest starting point. Being consistent with what your identity is additionally about being straightforward with your better half and that helps manufacture a confiding in relationship.

CHAPTER FIVE

Have some good times

Few out of every odd day of marriage is energizing. Incidentally, the fatigue sets in. You get into a daily practice and do very similar things all day every day. At the point when overlooked, weariness can prompt misery. So what do you do? Have a good time and don't let weariness creep into your relationship. Go on dates, picnics, travels and visits. Or on the other hand plan film evenings, cook supper together, watch a television arrangement, be senseless together, take yoga or move classes together, become familiar with a language together and accomplish something that will help both of you escape your usual ranges of familiarity.

Venture up the sentiment

Relationships that need sentiment will in general burn out sometime. So step up your sentiment by an indent or two and start again from scratch. Get coy, bother him, contact him affectionately, kiss him unexpectedly and lead him in the room. Venturing out sentiment or lovemaking doesn't mean you are poor and it won't make you any not exactly the man. So in case you're in the state of mind for something sentimental, feel free to do it. Shock him!

15. Get innovative in bed

One thing that all men need to know is that they are acceptable in bed. They have to hear it frequently, to support their certainty and cause them to feel like 'da man'. All things considered, most men may not be open to asking what they need in bed. In any case, in a marriage, you ought to have the option to discuss your most stunning dreams and give them a shot. Along these lines, don't stress over getting imaginative and taking a stab at something new with your significant other. It could be something that you like, or he enjoys. Get it done without stressing over being judged.

CHAPTER SIX

CONCLUTION

Being a decent spouse isn't tied in with being an accommodating or submissive wife that obliges each need of her significant other (hi! This isn't the '50s). It is tied in with being the ideal accomplice who contributes similarly to the relationship and supplements the spouse's character. Relationships are shared, so on the off chance that you need a decent spouse, you must be happy to be a decent wife.